BETTER SELF-ESTEEM

REENTRY
ESSENTIALS, INC.

Life Skills Series
Basic Skills for Lifelong Success

This workbook belongs to:

_____

You may find it helpful to keep important names and phone numbers handy.

Write them below.

Primary health-care provider

Name_____

Phone_____

Other health-care providers

Name_____

Phone_____

Health plan

Name_____

Phone_____

Pharmacy

Name_____

Phone_____

An emergency contact

Name_____

Phone_____

Other important numbers

_____

_____

_____

_____

_____

_____

_____

_____

_____

_____

Reentry Essentials, Inc.
98 4th Street, Suite 414
Brooklyn, NY 11231
P: 347.973.0004
E: info@ReentryEssentials.org
I: www.ReentryEssentials.org

BETTER SELF-ESTEEM COULD HELP MAKE YOUR LIFE BETTER.

If you're looking to improve your self-esteem, this workbook is for you. It has information and activities to help you:

Learn what it means to have high self-esteem

—and why it is important.

See how your self-esteem is affecting your life

—and learn about changes you can make to improve how you feel about yourself.

Start building your self-esteem

—so you can live a more enjoyable, satisfying life.

Use this workbook in the way that works best for you.

You may want to use it over many months or longer. You may want to do the activities in a different order than they are given here—or keep coming back to them as things change.

Improving self-esteem takes time and effort. But the rewards are worth it!

CONTENT

What is self-esteem? 3

Having high self-esteem helps you get the most out of life. 4

Having low self-esteem makes life less satisfying............. 5

Low self-esteem often exists together with other problems. 6

Assessing your self-esteem is the first step in changing it. 7

Self-esteem checklist 8

Possible sources of low self-esteem 9

Self-esteem journal 10

You can change how you feel about yourself. 11

Think about your negative and positive self-views.......... 12

Changing also involves knowing your strengths and weaknesses. 13

Strengths and weaknesses... 14

Silence your inner critic. 15

Practice positive self-talk... 16

Communicating assertively... 17

Practice assertive communication. 18

Keep improving your skills and knowledge. 19

Make a plan... 20

Do good things for yourself.. 21

What good things can you do for yourself?..................... 22

Build a circle of support. 23

Be a source of support, too... 24

Map out your circle of support. 25

Start setting some realistic goals. 26

My goals for the next few days, weeks or months 27

My longer term goals.. 28

Consider seeking professional help. 29

Add high self-esteem to your other good qualities! 30

WHAT IS SELF-ESTEEM?

It's how you feel about yourself—about your worth as a person and your ability to meet life's challenges.

A person may have many different feelings about him or herself, depending on:

The different roles he or she plays in life

For example, a person may have different feelings about his or her worth and abilities:

- At work—some people are confident at work and do not question their future there, while others may feel insecure and often worry if they will keep their job.
- At home—some people feel competent and secure in their home life, while others feel they cannot manage their relationships or responsibilities as well as they "should."
- At school—some people may enjoy the academic and/or social challenges at school, while others lack confidence in their abilities.
- At social events—some people may feel comfortable around lots of people, while others have trouble starting conversations.

The same person who feels confident in one setting may feel insecure in another.

His or her varied personal qualities

For example, a person may have different feelings about his or her:

- Appearance—some people are confident in how they look, while others focus on what they see as "flaws" in their appearance.
- Intelligence—some people are confident in their knowledge, while others feel self-conscious about how much they know or how much education they've had.
- Romantic appeal—some people may see themselves as attractive, while others may feel no one would be interested in them.

Again, the same people who feel confident in one area may feel less so in another. For example, someone may feel he or she is smart, but not attractive.

Your self-esteem is made up of these many different views.

The more positive views you have, the higher your self-esteem. Many people are used to focusing so much on what they don't like about themselves that they forget they have many positive qualities. This workbook will help you take a closer look at all of your positive qualities— and learn to celebrate them!

It is difficult to make a man miserable while he feels worthy of himself...

Abraham Lincoln

HAVING HIGH SELF-ESTEEM HELPS YOU GET THE MOST OUT OF LIFE.

It can help you:

Meet challenges

When you believe in yourself, you are more likely to:

- add new challenges as you meet old ones
- take risks and develop your abilities
- try new things

Value yourself

To value yourself means to know that you matter, despite any mistakes you make or any weaknesses you have. Learning to value yourself involves looking for the things that make you you. You have unique qualities that make you special. Knowing what these are can help make you feel important—because you are!

Have better relationships

When you feel comfortable in your own skin, you're more likely to:

- feel comfortable around other people
- be more eager to meet new people—and develop closer relationships

Sometimes when people don't feel good about themselves, they allow other people to put them down or use them unfairly. People who value themselves are more likely to stand up for their rights so people don't take advantage of them.

Be flexible

Sometimes change can be scary. Feeling confident about yourself can make it easier to accept new ideas and ways of doing things.

Having high self-esteem does not mean having an ego that's too big.

It means being able to be honest with yourself about:

- your strengths and weaknesses
- changes you can— and want to—make
- what things you cannot change—or can accept as they are—so you can work on more important changes

Thinking about these can help you start raising your self-esteem to a healthy level.

I'm not afraid of storms, for I'm learning how to sail my ship.

Louisa May Alcott, Little Women

HAVING LOW SELF-ESTEEM MAKES LIFE LESS SATISFYING.
Low self-esteem can lead to:

Lack of confidence

People with low self-esteem often have little faith in their abilities. They tend to think that if they failed in the past, they are doomed to fail again. This can affect how they perform in school, at work and in other aspects of life.

Without confidence, people are less likely to take any risks or challenge themselves to try new things or meet new people.

Not reaching your full potential

People with low self-esteem may find themselves doing less than they are really able to do. For example, they may:

- not make an effort because they expect to fail
- have low expectations of themselves

Unhealthy relationships

People who feel bad about themselves tend to find it hard to develop close relationships. The result may be a lonely and unsatisfying personal life. People who feel bad about themselves are also less likely to stand up for themselves when others don't treat them fairly. This can lead to:

- poor work situations (others may take advantage of the person)
- poor personal relationships (family members or a spouse may not treat the person with respect if the person does not stand up for him—or herself

Pushing yourself too hard

Worrying about not being good enough can make people feel like they need to be perfect.

A distorted view of yourself and others

When people see themselves as failures, they don't give themselves credit for their accomplishments. They tend to think most people are "better" than they are. When people feel this way, they also tend to feel they don't deserve to be happy.

When people with low self-esteem compare themselves to others, they tend to focus on all the things the other person can do rather than their own unique abilities.

A man cannot be comfortable without his own approval.

Mark Twain

LOW SELF-ESTEEM OFTEN EXISTS TOGETHER WITH OTHER PROBLEMS.
These include:

Depression

Depression is a long-lasting unhappiness characterized by many symptoms, including feelings of worthlessness or hopelessness.

People who are depressed may avoid:

- work
- other people
- activities that used to be of interest

(See page 29 for symptoms of depression and when to seek help.)

Anxiety

People with an anxiety disorder and low self-esteem may feel worry, fear or panic. They may be afraid of making changes or trying new things. Anxiety disorders can include:

- panic attacks
- phobias (intense, irrational fears)
- obsessive-compulsive disorders

Trouble managing anger

The person may feel angry at him- or herself for not being "good enough." He or she may also feel angry at others—and feel worse about him- or herself because of it.

Problems with alcohol or other drug use

The person may turn to alcohol or other drugs to try to dull the painful feelings that are part of having low self-esteem. Having a problem with alcohol or other drugs may make a person feel worse about him—or herself.

Eating disorders

These include:

- anorexia nervosa
- bulimia nervosa

People with eating disorders often have negative feelings about their self-image or feel a lack of control. These feelings are also related to low self-esteem.

Getting help can improve your sense of self-worth.

If you have any of these problems or any other concerns, talk with your health-care provider. (See page 29 for other sources of help, too.) Talk about how your self-esteem and the problem may be affecting each other—and about treatments that can help. Use this space for questions and notes:

_____

_____

_____

_____

_____

_____

_____

_____

_____

_____

_____

_____

A higher self-esteem is worth working for

ASSESSING YOUR SELF-ESTEEM IS THE FIRST STEP IN CHANGING IT.

Think about how you view yourself.
These questions can help you get started. Write yes or no on the line after each question.

1. Do you feel easily hurt by criticism? _____
2. Are you very shy or too aggressive? _____
3. Do you hide how you feel from other people? _____
4. Are you afraid to have close relationships? _____
5. Do you try to blame your mistakes on other people? _____
6. Do you avoid trying positive new activities? _____
7. Do you wish you could change how you look? _____
8. Do you avoid sharing your personal successes with others? _____
9. Do you feel glad when other people fail? _____
10. Do you look for excuses not to change? _____

1. Do you accept polite, helpful criticism? _____
2. Do you feel comfortable meeting new people? _____
3. Do you share your feelings openly and honestly with others? _____
4. Do you value your close relationships? _____
5. Can you laugh at your mistakes, as well as learn from them? _____
6. Do you seek out and enjoy new challenges? _____
7. Are you happy with the way you look? _____
8. Do you give yourself credit for your achievements? _____
9. Do you feel happy for others when they succeed? _____
10. Do you accept changes in yourself as they occur? _____

If you answered most of these questions yes, your self-esteem could probably use improvement.

If you answered most of these questions yes, you probably have a healthy opinion of yourself.

Think about possible sources of your feelings.

A person's self-esteem is first formed in childhood. People who have low self-esteem often see relationships and events in terms of past experiences. For example, a person may not feel his or her opinions matter if, as a child, he or she:

- was criticized often for what he or she said
- often did not receive attention when he or she spoke

Thinking about possible sources of your feelings can help you start separating past experiences from events and relationships in your life now.

Fill in the worksheet on the next page.

See how your answers change when you view yourself in different roles, such as a parent or friend. Why do you think your self-esteem changes in different situations?

SELF-ESTEEM CHECKLIST

Put a check in the box next to each statement that best describes how you view yourself when it comes to different areas in your life. Does your view of yourself differ by area?

I Am	As a Parent			As An Employee			As a Friend			As a Partner In a Relationship		
	Agree	Neutral	Disagree	Agree	Neutral	Disagree	Agree	Neutral	Disagree	Agree	Neutral	Disagree
Smart	☐	☐	☐	☐	☐	☐	☐	☐	☐	☐	☐	☐
Able to Accomplish Things	☐	☐	☐	☐	☐	☐	☐	☐	☐	☐	☐	☐
Likable	☐	☐	☐	☐	☐	☐	☐	☐	☐	☐	☐	☐
Able to Ask For What I Want/Need	☐	☐	☐	☐	☐	☐	☐	☐	☐	☐	☐	☐
A Person With Strong Morals	☐	☐	☐	☐	☐	☐	☐	☐	☐	☐	☐	☐
Deserving of Respect From Others	☐	☐	☐	☐	☐	☐	☐	☐	☐	☐	☐	☐

Statements you marked as "disagree" or "neutral" show where higher self-esteem could help. Use your answers to think about what you want to try improving first.

POSSIBLE SOURCES OF LOW SELF-ESTEEM

Think about areas of your life where you feel you have low self-esteem, and what the possible sources might be. You can fill out this worksheet over time, as things occur to you.

Feelings of low self-esteem	Possible source(s)
Examples:	Examples:
I feel like a failure if I do not do everything just right.	When I was a child, my mistakes always got more notice than what I did right. I feel like I have to be perfect to have others' approval.
I avoid situations where I have to meet people—If I feel like they would rather be talking to someone else.	As a child, other kids called me fat a lot. I feel like I should have a perfect body for other people to want to be with me.

SELF-ESTEEM JOURNAL

Keep a journal to track your self-esteem.

This can:

- help you see how you tend to view yourself in certain situations and roles
- help you keep noticing and improving negative self-views
- help you maintain positive self-views

Use this journal to keep track of times when you are feeling low self-esteem and times when you are feeling good about yourself.

In the Notes sections, include information that may help you see patterns. For example, do you often feel better or worse about yourself after a specific activity? Write down where you were, what was happening or being said, who was there, etc.

Try using this journal for a week or two to start with. Keep using it for as long as you find it helpful.

Date _____

How I felt _____

Notes _____

_____

_____

Date _____

How I felt _____

Notes _____

_____

_____

Date _____

How I felt _____

Notes _____

_____

_____

Date _____

How I felt _____

Notes _____

_____

_____

YOU CAN CHANGE HOW YOU FEEL ABOUT YOURSELF.

It's not easy and it won't happen right away. But breaking the process into parts can help you take control. 2 key steps are to:

1. Identify negative views you have about yourself.

For example, people with low self-esteem often believe that they are "stupid" or "ugly." They may:

• see these beliefs as true in all situations and in everyone's eyes

• let the beliefs affect what they do and how they act toward others

Negative views can be very subtle. You may not even recognize them as negative. For example, some people naturally put themselves down because they don't want others to think they think too highly of themselves. But after a while, they may start to believe those put-downs.

The truth is, people are usually drawn to those who feel good about themselves and have a positive outlook. Remember, there is a difference between feeling good about yourself and being arrogant. It's OK to have pride in your accomplishments!

2. Identify your positive self-views.

Examples include seeing yourself as being kind and reliable. When you have low self-esteem:

- It may be hard to accept or express positive views about yourself. But remember, there is nothing wrong with feeling good about the things you do!
- It may help to involve family and friends who can help you see and accept these views. Ask them to tell you the things they like about you. Be sure to have them give you specific things they like and why. For example, they may say they enjoy your company because you are a good listener and have good ideas.

Be sure to write down what your friends and family tell you. Save what you write and reread it from time to time to remind you how special people think you are—and why.

Being aware of your self-views can help you see a truer picture of yourself.

For example:

- It can help you see how your negative self-views affect your life. When you can see how each specific view affects how you feel, you can start working on changing each one.
- It can help you focus on your positive self-views and how you can use these to improve your overall view of yourself. For example, let's say one positive view you have is "I like the way I help others." You could make a list of all the ways you've helped. That can help you see how much you've made a change in other people's lives. That's something to feel good about!

No one can make you feel inferior without your consent.

Eleanor Roosevelt

THINK ABOUT YOUR NEGATIVE AND POSITIVE SELF-VIEWS.

Use this page to list them.

You may discover some of these views as you keep your journal. Add others as they occur to you.

Each time you write down a negative self-view ask yourself:

- Is this really true?
- Why do I think this?

Then review your list of positive self-views. Ask yourself:

- Which of these views am I most proud of?
- How can I apply these qualities on a regular basis to help change my negative self-views?

Negative self-views

Examples:

"No one could like me."

"I'm never good enough at anything I do."

_____

_____

_____

_____

_____

_____

_____

Positive self-views

Examples:

"I am caring and respectful."

"I am a hard worker."

_____

_____

_____

_____

_____

_____

_____

_____

_____

CHANGING ALSO INVOLVES KNOWING YOUR STRENGTHS AND WEAKNESSES.

Everyone has skills and talents.

For example, a person may manage time well, cook well or be good at fixing cars. But if you have low self-esteem, you:

- may not see your own strengths—or not see them as anything special
- may need others to help you see your strengths and accept their value

When you're thinking about possible strengths, remember that it is OK to take pride in what you can do well! Think about:

- general things you are good at, such as being kind to others and being generous
- specific things you are good at, such as being able to play an instrument, having a knack for remembering specific details or statistics, or being able to cook a certain meal well

Be proud of ALL of your strengths, both big and small.

Everyone has weaknesses, too.

For example, a person may not be good at using computers or at talking with people he or she does not know well. Thinking about your weaknesses can help you decide:

- which ones you want to try changing
- which ones you cannot change or can accept as OK

Most people have things about themselves that they can't change. For example, someone may not like his or her voice or height. But often there are things we don't like that we can change. For example, if a person wants to improve:

- computer skills, he or she could ask a friend to help or take a class
- social skills, he or she could take steps to slowly meet more people and participate in social activities. (Professional help is also available to improve these skills)

Your self-views, strengths and weaknesses can all affect each other.

For example:

- Someone who views him or herself as "stupid" may see losing a word game as "proof." The person may not think about the ways he or she is smart (for example, understanding how cars work).
- Someone who views him- or herself as not likable may avoid meeting people. This keeps him or her from having chances to exercise important social skills, even though he or she may have the qualities that make a very good friend.

The purpose of life is undoubtedly to know oneself.

Mohandas Gandhi

STRENGTHS AND WEAKNESSES

Start thinking about what your strengths and weaknesses are.

Write them down and add others as they occur to you. What you write here can also help you fill out the worksheet on page 16.

When you're thinking about your strengths:

- try to list as many as you can— even things you think are "small"
- consider your daily routine to help you come up with strengths you take for granted. (For example, you may be a good driver, great at making breakfast or friendly to your co-workers)

When you're thinking about your weaknesses, think about ways you might use your strengths to improve them. For example, "The next time I lose my patience with someone, I will try to use my strong listening skills to get the full story before I pass judgment."

Strengths

Examples:

"I am a good listener."
"I know a lot about current events."

_____

_____

_____

_____

_____

_____

_____

_____

_____

_____

Weaknesses

Examples:

"Sometimes I lose my patience too quickly."
"I put off tasks I don't look forward to. I miss some work deadlines because of it. "

_____

_____

_____

_____

_____

_____

_____

SILENCE YOUR INNER CRITIC.

Start changing your negative views by using positive self-talk.

Be aware of your inner negative voice.

Everyone has one. In people with low self-esteem, this voice can be very harsh. It is the voice that:

- criticizes and judges you— for example, "I'm so dumb, I'll never get that job."
- blames you for things— for example, "I didn't prepare enough for that job interview. I blew it!"
- tells you that you are not good enough—for example, "I didn't answer the questions well. I'll never get that job!"
- makes your weaknesses seem worse than they are, for example, "My computer skills are so bad that no one will ever hire me!"
- compares you negatively to others—for example, "The other applicants are probably way more qualified than I am."

Start replacing negative talk with positive, realistic messages.

To do this, put a stop to the negative thought and replace it with a positive one. For example:

- "Saying that I'm too stupid for this job is a way to avoid applying, so I won't have to face a possible rejection. I can't get a new job if I don't try."
- "That interview was challenging, but I know I did my best. If I don't get the job, the interview was good practice for my next try."
- "My computer skills aren't the best—but they aren't the worst, either. If they aren't good enough for a job I want, I can take steps to improve them."
- "This job probably had a lot of applicants. There may be some who are more qualified than I am, but I know I met the requirements on the application and did my best to present my skills."

For some people, their negative voice has been talking to them for a long time!

Replacing it with a positive, encouraging voice takes practice.

Remember, the first step in silencing your negative voice is to start noticing all of the negative thoughts you have about yourself. Then, start working on ways to replace each one with a statement that is more accurate— and positive. If there truly is something about yourself that you aren't happy about, think of positive ways you can change it.

I believe that it is harder still to be just toward oneself than toward others.

Andre Gide

PRACTICE POSITIVE SELF-TALK.

Look at what you wrote on the earlier worksheets (pages 7-10, 12 and 14) to help you start on this key step. Write down your most common examples of negative self-talk. Add others as you notice them. Next to each one, write a positive, realistic statement to say instead. Practice using the positive statements when you hear yourself saying the negative ones.

Negative self-talk	Positive self-talk to replace it with
Examples:	Examples:
"I hate how my chin looks. I'm so ugly."	"I do have a big chin. But I'm not ugly just because I don't fit some perfect ideal. And I have nice eyes and hair."
"I'm too boring. If I go to that party, no one will want to talk to me anyway."	"I am quiet and not great at small talk. But I'm not boring. People seem interested in me when I join the lunch conversations at work."

COMMUNICATING ASSERTIVELY

Expressing wants and needs can be hard when you have feelings of low self-esteem—but with practice, you can communicate with confidence.

Understand what assertive communication is.

Being assertive means expressing your feelings in a way that doesn't blame others—or yourself. It also means you express yourself in a clear, firm way, rather than agreeing with what someone else says just to avoid conflict.

Leaning to communicate assertively can help you:

- build better friendships—they're good for your self-esteem
- avoid or settle conflicts with relatives, friends and co-workers—unresolved conflicts can make you feel bad about yourself and contribute to low self-esteem
- learn about people and their feelings—assertive communication involves listening as well as speaking

Use "I" statements.

These can help you avoid sounding like you are blaming or criticizing. The other person may be more open to what you have to say. For example:

- Don't say, "You're such a jerk for making fun of the way I talk."
- Say, "I feel hurt when you make fun of the way I talk."

State what you feel, think and want.

For example, say, "I know you may just think of it as joking. But I feel put down when I talk about something and your only response is to make fun of how I say it. It makes me think what I have to say doesn't matter to you. I'd really like it if you could respond to the point I'm making instead."

Ask the person for a response.

For example, say, "I think we could have some good talks about things if you could do this. Do you think you could try it?"

Use body language that helps show you mean what you say.

Possible ways to do this include:

- making eye contact
- standing in a confident pose (not wringing your hands, for example).

Use a confident tone of voice, too. But be careful not to look or sound like you're attacking the other person.

Many things are lost for want of asking.

George Herbert

PRACTICE ASSERTIVE COMMUNICATION.

How can you be assertive in your daily conversations?

Think of some things you want to ask for and the people you want to ask. Write what you could say in the space provided. You may want to practice asking in front of a mirror so you can check your body language.

Don't forget to listen.

Listening is more than just hearing. It is a skill you have to practice, just like speaking. Active listening means:

- looking at the person
- not interrupting
- paying attention—not thinking about what you want to say in reply

When the person is finished, summarize what you've heard in your own words to show you've listened and understood.

What I want (and from whom)

Example: Help from family members with keeping the house neat

Possible statement

Example: I feel discouraged when I find things lying around after cleaning up. I'd really like a neat house and this makes me think that what I want doesn't matter. Can we come up with a way for you to help more with picking up?

What I want (and from whom):

Possible statement:

What I want (and from whom):

Possible statement:

KEEP IMPROVING YOUR SKILLS AND KNOWLEDGE.

Accomplishing things—even the effort itself—can help you feel better about yourself. Ask yourself:

What skills and knowledge do I already have?

Think about all the roles you play, and what it takes to do these. Possible examples include:

- doing certain kinds of math, if you regularly do food shopping on a budget
- working with your hands, if you have a hobby or a job that requires it
- organizing people to get tasks done, if this is part of your home or work routine

Remember, you probably have many more skills than you realize! If you have trouble coming up with skills, think about all the things you do each day, at home and at work. Make a list of all of your daily responsibilities and what skills are required to carry them out. For example:

- Do you help family members get ready for work and school? Then you have good organizational skills!
- Do you pay bills? Then you have math skills!

What new skills and knowledge would I like to develop?

Think about things you may have wanted to try, but never have. Perhaps you keep telling yourself you wouldn't be good at them. Remind yourself that things you enjoy are worth doing, even if you are not as good at them as you think you should be. For example, perhaps you've thought about:

- learning to dance
- joining a summer softball league
- being involved in community theater
- volunteering for a community organization

In addition to new things, think of some skills you already have that you'd like to improve. For example, if you are skilled at cooking a certain meal, maybe you'd like to learn new cooking techniques so that you can expand on what you can make for yourself and others.

How will these skills help me feel better about myself and improve my life?

When thinking about things you'd like to try, learn or improve, think also about how they might improve your daily life. For example:

- learning to play an instrument may help you relax after a busy day, or help you meet new people if you perform or practice with a group
- volunteering can help you feel good about yourself as well as help you meet other people and make a difference in your community

Few (are) too young, and none too old, to make the attempt to learn.

Booker T. Washington

MAKE A PLAN.

Think about specific skills or interests you would like to improve and develop.

Write them in the space provided. Include any areas you want to learn more about, too.

For each one, think about small steps you could take to carry these out. Write the steps down. Be sure to make each step something that is not too overwhelming. Like any big job or goal, you are more likely to succeed if you plan it out into reasonable steps that make sense for you.

Celebrate your success at every step!

Skill/knowledge/interest

Example: Join a summer softball league next season.

Steps

Example: 1. Ask Pat to join with me. 2. Go watch some games together this season and practice ahead of time. 3. Ask the coach or players about the league.

Skill/knowledge/interest:

_____

_____

_____

_____

Steps:

_____

_____

_____

_____

Skill/knowledge/interest:

_____

_____

_____

_____

Steps:

_____

_____

_____

_____

DO GOOD THINGS FOR YOURSELF.

It's important to meet your emotional needs and other needs. Like other steps you take to improve your self-esteem, this can take practice.

It can be easy to think that only others deserve good things.

When you have low self-esteem, you may think that:

- you don't deserve good things or haven't done anything worth rewarding yourself for
- you should devote your time to others' needs

Keep reminding yourself that you would want others you care about to have good things—and that you deserve them just like they do.

Being good to yourself can help change how you feel.

Over time, you'll start feeling like being good to yourself is more natural and acceptable.

Think about things you may enjoy doing.

For example, you may enjoy:

- relaxing in a hot bath after a busy day
- spending an evening out with friends
- putting chores on hold to take a walk on a beautiful day
- having a good talk with a family member or close friend
- shopping for a new outfit, music CD, etc.

Plan to try one or two enjoyable activities every week or two.

Think about what makes you happy.

In addition to activities like the ones described above, think also about the general things that make you happy and how you can expose yourself to these things more often. Even something as simple as listening to music more often can make a difference.

Take good care of yourself.

It's easy to overlook doing the things that make us feel good in body and mind. But healthy daily habits can improve how we feel inside and out. For example:

- Eat well. A healthy, balanced diet can improve your overall health and make you feel good about yourself. Visit www.ChooseMyPlate.gov for details on a diet that's right for you.
- Stay active. Regular physical activity can give you more energy and help you stay physically fit. (Talk to a healthcare provider before starting an exercise program.)
- Get plenty of sleep. Being well rested can help you have more energy throughout the day.
- Practice good personal hygiene. Keeping up your appearance shows you care about yourself.

It is a happy talent to know how to play.

Ralph Waldo Emerson

WHAT GOOD THINGS CAN YOU DO FOR YOURSELF?
Make a plan!

Follow these steps:

- In the left-hand column, write as many things that you enjoy as you can think of (include things that don't cost a lot).
- Number each activity in order of importance to you.
- In the right-hand column, make a plan for doing each of your 3-5 top activities.

- Write about it! Once you've carried out your plan, write about the activity and how it made you feel. You can write in a journal or notebook. Keep your entries to remind you of your experience—and to inspire you to do it again!

I enjoy...

Example: Turning on the music and singing along

I enjoy...

Example: Going to the movies with my best friend

I enjoy...

_____

_____

_____

_____

_____

_____

_____

_____

_____

_____

_____

_____

_____

I plan to...

Example: Take 10 minutes to listen to music when I get home from work

I plan to...

Example: Schedule a "date" with my friend to see a movie once a month

I plan to...

_____

_____

_____

_____

_____

_____

_____

_____

_____

_____

_____

_____

_____

BUILD A CIRCLE OF SUPPORT.
Support from others is vital to having high self-esteem.
Here are some ways to build a support network:

Work to improve existing relationships.

People with low self-esteem often give a lot without asking for anything in return. They also judge themselves by others' standards. It's important that others:

- show love and acceptance toward you
- give you credit for what you do
- respect you

One way to help improve relationships is to be assertive (review pages 17-18). When you are assertive, you help keep yourself from being taken advantage of.

Being assertive can also help you feel better about yourself. For example, sharing your true feelings rather than agreeing with someone to avoid an argument can help you feel strong and sure of yourself. People are more likely to respect you when you stand up for what you believe in, even if they don't agree with you.

Try making some new friends.

Think about whether you might benefit from having a wider circle of support. You might try:

- meeting others with similar interests—for example, by taking a class or through a community or religious organization
- joining or starting a support group that focuses on self-growth. For information, try asking your health-care provider or checking your local newspaper or phone book

Avoid people who don't respect you.

You don't need to be friends with everyone. Avoid people who don't listen to you or who take advantage of you. You deserve friends who are willing to give you the same respect you show to them.

Ask others to help you improve your self-esteem.

Think of friends, family members and others from different areas of your life whom you feel could be helpful. Ask them to encourage and support your efforts. For example:

- Share your list of good things you'd like to do for yourself, and ask them to participate with you (if any of the activities involve others).
- Talk about skills you'd like to improve and ask them to help you track your progress and offer encouragement.
- Ask them to help you recognize times when you put yourself down or don't act assertively.

Asking for help is not a sign of weakness. It shows you care enough about yourself to want to make a change for the better!

I felt it shelter to speak to you.

Emily Dickinson

BE A SOURCE OF SUPPORT. TOO.

Be positive toward others.

Having negative feelings about yourself can lead to having these same feelings about others.

Try to:

- Avoid criticizing, judging or blaming other people.
- Understand others' feelings and views.
- Be a good listener. Pay attention without judging while others talk. You don't have to agree with the person, but it's important to respect other people's points of view.
- Offer encouragement and support to others. Point out their strengths and positive qualities.
- Be accepting of flaws and mistakes.
- Forgive others for past hurts. Focus on the present and future.

Being positive toward others can help you feel more positive about yourself, too.

Help others improve their self-esteem.

If you know someone who may benefit from what you've learned about self-esteem, share your knowledge.

Talk about ways you plan to improve your self-esteem and whether those steps might help the person. Discuss how you might help each other and take these steps together.

Along with the tips above, you can also help the person by:

- showing an interest in the person (by asking questions about him or her, for example)
- expressing your belief in the person's ability to achieve goals and make changes
- talking with—and listening to— the person to show you care

Helping others feels good!

There are other ways to help others—and help yourself! When you take the time to help others, it shows you value yourself. You have something to give!

Think about ways you might be able to help others in your life. For example, consider:

- spending time with someone who lives alone, such as an older relative or friend— you could share a meal, read to the person, or simply be there to talk
- volunteering your time at a place that could benefit from the help of people with different skills—for example, a hospital, nursing home or soup kitchen
- offering to help someone in need, such as someone who needs transportation somewhere or help with housework

MAP OUT YOUR CIRCLE OF SUPPORT.

Write your name in the small circle. Outside the big circle, write the names of people who could give you support. For each person, draw a line to your name and write how he or she could help. You may also want to write names and phone numbers on the inside front cover.

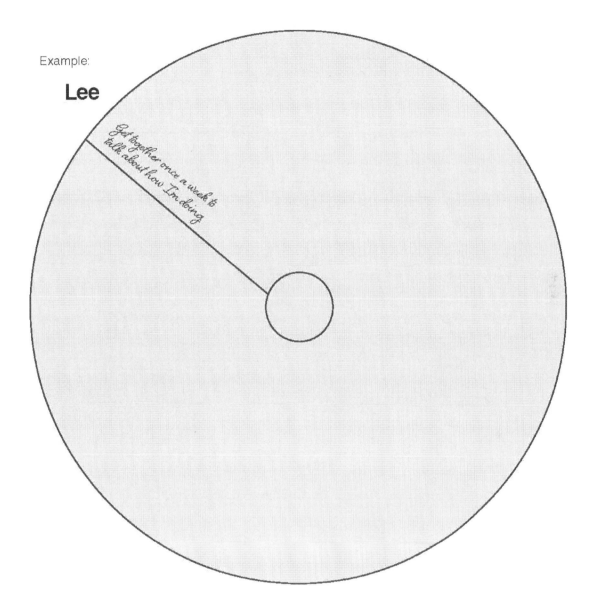

Example:

Lee

Get together once a week to talk about how I'm doing

You may also want to make a map showing the support you can give others. Or you can include the information in this map, using a different color.

START SETTING SOME REALISTIC GOALS.

Set goals for the next few days, weeks or months.

These are called short-term goals. Meeting these goals can help you feel more confident about setting and meeting longer-term goals. Here are some examples.

- "For the next 3 days, I'll call 1 community organization a day to ask about volunteering."
- "For the next week, I'll look into clubs or classes offered in my community that I might enjoy."
- "For the next month, I'll write down every time I notice myself thinking I'm stupid. I'll write something helpful to say instead."

When making goals, look over the lists you made earlier of your strengths and weaknesses and the things you enjoy. Try to choose goals that will help you improve the areas you want to work on or do things you enjoy.

Set some longer term goals, too.

Starting to think about these can help you decide on shorter term goals to start with and to keep setting more along the way. For example, the short term goals listed to the left may be steps toward a larger goal. Here is how the next step might look for each example:

- "I'll attend the next volunteer training at an organization whose work interests me."
- "I'll choose a group or class to sign up for and make a commitment to try it for at least 1 month."
- "I'll be able to stop telling myself I'm stupid by 4 months from now."

To help you stay motivated:

- Keep goals realistic. Make them specific. For example, say "I want to do 2 fun things each week," instead of "I want to have more fun." Think about what you will need (money, time, etc.) to meet the goal.
- Aim to make just 1-2 changes at a time.
- Celebrate your achievements. For example, go out with friends after reaching a certain goal.
- Avoid judging yourself if you fail to reach a goal. Instead, focus on what you achieved along the way and what you might want to try doing differently.

To climb steep hills requires slow pace at first.

William Shakespeare, Henry the Eighth

MY GOALS FOR THE NEXT FEW DAYS. WEEKS OR MONTHS

Set 1-2 short-term goals. Remember to follow the tips on page 26. In the Notes section, write down information such as how your progress is going, changes you may want to make in the goal, when you achieved it and what goal to set next.

Goal	Time frame/needs for meeting it	Notes
Examples:	Examples:	Examples:
For 1 week, start 1 conversation a day with a co-worker during lunch.	1 week for ½ hour each day–I'll try to sit with people at lunch rather than by myself	The first few days, the person seemed rushed. I did not take it personally. Today, I had a nice talk with the person about our recent vacations
For 1 week, say something positive about myself every morning.	1 week for 5 minutes each morning remind myself of the positive thing throughout the day.	I was able to find something to say every day. I felt better about facing the day.

MY LONGER TERM GOALS

Start thinking now about what some of these might be.
Keep them in mind as you set shorter-term goals.

Goal	Time frame/needs for meeting it	Notes
Examples: Talk more with co-workers during lunch.	Examples: 3 months	Examples: Good progress in the last 2 months. I still get nervous with someone I don't know well. May need to continue shorter-term goals a little longer
Stop putting myself down and focus on the positive.	2 months	Doing well, but sometimes I still blame myself when things go wrong, even if it wasn't my fault. I need to keep working on this.

CONSIDER SEEKING PROFESSIONAL HELP.

This may help you have more success more quickly.

You may be able to do a lot on your own and with the support of family and friends. Review pages 23-24, and go over your support circle on page 25.

You may also find it helpful to talk with:

- your health-care provider
- a therapist, counselor or other mental health professional
- a religious or spiritual leader

If you are not sure where to find help, start by contacting your health-care provider or local hospital. Use this space for notes:

_____

_____

_____

_____

_____

Remember—asking for help is not a sign of weakness. It means you care enough about yourself to improve your overall wellness. And that's a sign of improved self-esteem!

Know when professional help may be needed.

Possible signs include:

• having low self-confidence for a prolonged period of time

• having frequent mood changes

• feeling no improvement after making your own efforts

You may find that you can do some things on your own but need help doing other things. If you have any questions or concerns about your efforts, talk with your health-care provider.

It can be no dishonor to learn from others when they speak good sense.

Sophocles, Antigone

Be alert for signs of serious problems, such as depression.

Signs of depression include:

- persistent sadness or irritability
- inability to enjoy activities that were once enjoyable, such as work, hobbies or sex
- a sense of hopelessness or guilt
- anxiety or restlessness
- trouble concentrating or remembering things
- trouble sleeping, or sleeping too much
- unexplained headaches, backaches or stomachaches
- eating too much or too little
- low energy
- thoughts of death or suicide (see below)

Most people have some of these symptoms from time to time, but if symptoms occur nearly every day for 2 weeks or longer, may be a sign of depression. Talk with your health-care provider if you think you may be depressed.

If you or someone you know has thoughts of suicide, seek help immediately by calling 9-1-1 or your local medical emergency number.

ADD HIGH SELF-ESTEEM TO YOUR OTHER GOOD QUALITIES!
Start taking steps day by day:

Keep focusing on your strengths.

Accept your weaknesses, too. Set goals to improve the ones you want to change, if it's possible to change them.

Work to make your relationships more satisfying.

Keep practicing assertive communication skills and being positive toward others.

Take pride in your accomplishments and efforts.

Give yourself credit for the things that you do well and work hard at.

Keep learning about self-esteem and how to improve it.

For more information:

- Ask your health-care provider or your local health clinic or hospital.
- Check at your local library or bookstore. Ask for help finding books or other materials.

Imagine all that a higher self-esteem can do for you. Enjoy your efforts and results—enjoy life!

Made in the USA
Columbia, SC
14 October 2024

43666953R00020